IT'S TIME
TO
CHANGE

IT'S TIME
TO
CHANGE

SYLVIE AYA ATTIA

Table of Contents

INTRODUCTION 7

IDENTITY 14

HISTORY 21

PRESENT 28

TAKING ACTION 34

A COMMON GOAL 41

TEAMWORK 48

VALUES 53

A SYSTEM 60

RESPECT 64

REPROGRAMMING 70

PRACTICAL ADVISES/CONCLUSION 78

INTRODUCTION

What do you see when you look at yourself in the mirror?

How do you see yourself? And how do you see people who look like you?

The answers to those questions are very important in understanding why you do the things you do.

With that being said, changing the way you perceive yourself can have a significant impact on how you behave and treat others.

There is a correlation between how one perceives themselves and their behavior.

The way we perceive ourselves influences the decisions we make, and the decisions we make affect our everyday lives and others. In reality, most people with a positive perception of themselves tend to be very positive, successful, and overcome. On the other hand, those who have a poor opinion of themselves tend to be very unhappy and hateful.

As a matter of fact, the "Doll Test", a study conducted to test the racial perceptions of young children, was done with a group of melanated children under 12 years old. Each child was given three dolls and instructed to select the most aesthetically pleasing one; however, most opted for dolls that did not resemble them. Very sad, isn't it? Why would these children feel like dolls that looked like them were not as pretty as the others? How did they come to that conclusion?

Society, culture, personal experiences, and the media often influence how we view ourselves.

Most people use criteria set by a system that may not reflect reality. What is reality?

Most philosophers define reality as what a person thinks is true. One's reality may differ from someone else's.

We live in a world filled with hatred, division, and violence, possibly because many people have the wrong concept of who they are.

This misconception, which pushes them to misjudge and discriminate against each other, further divides them.

All of that has to stop if we want to live in a better world. Division and ignorance are enemies to progress.

Knowledge is essential in fighting against division and ignorance since people are usually afraid of what they don't have knowledge of or understand. Differences are not always negative. They can actually be beneficial if we learn how to work with them.

The world is like a garden with different plants and flowers. Each one serves a specific purpose.

We are different in one or many ways, but that should not stop us from accepting each other. We are not to judge anyone, mainly when no one chose to be born African, European, African American, Caribbean, or Asian,... It was God's choice and purpose for each one of us. It's unfair to be angry at someone or hate people for their origin or skin color. People should not be blamed for the mistakes of their ancestors if they don't follow in their forefathers' footsteps.

Yes, so many things happened. Many abominable and painful things were done. So much hurt, so many lies! We cannot change the past, but we can change our present and future.

It's very important to leave the past behind and move forward, ensuring not to repeat the same mistakes. And please, let's keep in mind that all human beings are equal by principle or nature.

No one should feel superior to or better than anyone, especially for something they did not earn or work to get. It's unfair, nor does it make any sense! People usually denigrate others for lack of confidence. There is no need to prove who we are when we are sure of our identity.

Be happy with who you are, regardless of your skin color or origin.

IDENTITY

Anyone needs to know their true identity.

How you value yourself or how people see you may differ from your true identity.

I've seen too many children from the diaspora pretending to be what they are not. They had to work hard to fit in or be accepted by their peers or classmates. Not easy for them! Can you imagine constantly being bullied, laughed at, or misjudged because you're a little different?

So many people all over the world are being mistreated because the wrong identities were given to them.

A troubling pattern has emerged world-wide, where countless individuals are subjected to mistreatment due to the misrepresentation of their identities. Among the groups that have borne the brunt of this injustice are people with darker skin tones, who have faced disproportionate levels of discrimination and continue to experience ongoing obstacles.

True identity is relevant.

Now is the moment to challenge the false narratives and stereotypes imposed upon specific individuals so that we can shatter the chains of ignorance and confusion.

Knowing our true identity is paramount, particularly in light of the numerous lies spread about our history, nature, and purpose. Since all black people are connected to Africa, the

"Mother Land," a false and poor image of Africa, would give a bad image to black people. Being black is not a curse!

We are melanated people. Melanin is a pigment produced within the skin in cells called melanocytes, the primary determinant of skin color, eye color, and hair texture. Melanin preserves our skin from the sun's harmful ultra-violet rays. This pigment protects our skin from skin cancer. The different degrees of skin color are due to the amount of melanin, which is naturally stimulated once exposed to sunlight.

Melanin is important. Some scientists even believe that melanin protects from early hearing loss.

In fact, it was worth far more than gold in November 2018.

There is so much to say about the pigment that gives us the color of our skin. We should embrace our nature and know that we are special people.

On the other hand, melanin can retain drugs and other chemical substances in cells for a long time. As a result, people with darker skin tones are more vulnerable to drugs and nicotine than less melanated people.

Okay, enough talking about melanin. My point is that being black is as beautiful as being from another race. And we all know that many people with darker complexions have had or are having some hard times because of their appearance. Let's be real here! Beauty comes from inside out.

It is essential to know your identity and embrace it. Everything has a purpose and meaning on earth.

Many people have an identity crisis. They think to be what they're not. We cannot ask a cat to bark or treat a lion like a cat, especially when starving. A cat is not a dog or a lion. A fish is not a shark.

Every living being has a specific role to play in maintaining the world's equilibrium. If we take the example of a coconut tree, it's not in its nature to bear fruits like berries or apples. Going against its natural disposition may lead to a sense of unfulfillment or discontentment, as it was not meant to serve that purpose.

I cannot emphasize enough the importance of knowing your true identity.

Your true identity will tend to surface because that's the real you, and that can cause confusion and frustration.

To fulfill our mission, we must know who we are and walk in it.

We must protect our cultural heritage, which is a part of our identity.

History will help us understand and connect us to our roots. Where do we come from? Who are we?

History helps us better understand the present and learn from past mistakes. But we should not dwell in the past or stay there. Life is a continuity.

Each one has a beautiful story to write despite their "make-believe" origin.

HISTORY

All Human Beings come from Africa, the Motherland. Recently, scientists discovered that all Human Beings came from one couple, a man and a woman, thousands of years ago. That love story happened in Africa, proving humankind was initially melanated. Some scientists have also traced the world's modern languages back to a single tongue, an ancestral language spoken in Africa thousands of years ago.

Everything started in Africa, even life; Africa gave birth to humankind. There is no doubt about that. Division and hatred have to stop. It's time to unite. The Motherland is calling her children back home. Home does not necessarily mean the physical continent of Africa, but those who want to return are welcome. Home also means Africa in one's heart, which means to be at peace with who you are, your roots, and your origin.

To progress in life, it is imperative to have a clear understanding of our identity and our history. Our thought patterns and actions are deeply rooted in the historical narrative that has been presented to us. Were we really savages in need of being subjugated?

It is crucial to acknowledge the fact that Africa was home to several great empires, including Egypt with its magnificent pyramids, and Timbuktu, which was once the center of the ancient Mali Empire and housed one of the world's earliest universities. Contrary to the notion of savagery, people from diverse parts of the world traveled to Africa to acquire knowledge and education.

We cannot unite if we don't understand why there is division and strife among our people. Why so much hatred for our people?

As a result, some even hate themselves to the point of denying their roots. Unbelievable! It's not because some people don't like you or don't appreciate you that something is wrong with you! People are entitled to their own opinion. You cannot allow someone else's false opinion of you to affect you to the point of rejecting yourself. God sees you differently. He loves you regardless of your gender, origin, and social condition.

If you don't love yourself, what you look like, and what you identify with, you will eventually hate those that look like you as they reflect what you hate, and all of that hatred will lead to strife and division.

Now we understand better what's going on!

A negative image of Africa was promoted. The intention behind spreading a false and manipulated image of Africa was for Black people to hate who they are. Many people don't even want to associate themselves with our Motherland.

Africa, the cradle of humanity, endured a vicious campaign of defamation. Our beloved Motherland suffered greatly, losing countless children to the cruel horrors of slavery and then being further weakened by the oppression of colonization.

Colonization is like telling someone you are not who you say you are: "*We will give you a new identity,*" and that's what Africa is fighting against; a new identity.

A new identity for Africa will also mean a new identity for her children. But what kind of identity? No one is to change anyone's identity; that's a fraud. Your purpose is hidden in your identity. And If you're uncertain about who you are, it may hinder your ability to achieve your life's purpose. Africa is the mother of humanity. Nature teaches us that a mother naturally protects her children and takes care of the well-being of her family. Archeology and most religious books prove this. Indeed, the Bible has many stories about the Israelites going to Egypt for provision and security. Africa has always been there for humankind.

If Africa falls, everyone and everything connected to her will also fall. Our Motherland has been fighting to stay alive for me, you, and the Human Race. Her ground holds countless mysteries and there is much more to learn about our history.

Africa needs us to unite and remain strong.

PRESENT

I noticed that Black people are the only ones not helping each other succeed, with the exception of a few.

There is no need to compete against each other. We need each other. The need to compete against each other comes from a slavery mentality. The mind has been conditioned to think that there is not enough for everyone, causing our people to compete against each other to survive rather than working together and be more fruitful.

We must break free from this survival mentality and embrace abundance. Find what you were created for and do it. Each person has a unique purpose to fulfilling, and by collaborating, we can achieve greater. Despite our diverse backgrounds, we can unite around common goals and minimize our differences. Rather than focusing on our divides, we should prioritize our collective accomplishments. To achieve this, we must accept our cultural differences. We are different, but the same people. We know the old strategy, *"Divide and conquer,"* or the famous Bible verse: *"Every city or house divided against itself will not stand."* Our differences shouldn't stop us from working together. In fact, we should take advantage of our unlikeliness.

Sometimes, what makes you different is what makes you unique. All human beings are special in a way and should accept one another despite their so-called origins. People should stop associating the color black with evil things.

Black was not associated with death before slavery and colonization in most African cultures. Black was associated with good and divine things. Every culture associates their god with the color of their skin and the way they look. People have to be able to relate to the God that they worship. Consequently, several religious scriptures, written works, and artworks were altered to conform to the cultural and societal standards of the community that adopted them.

Some fight about the color of our Messiah, Yeshua, called Jesus in many cultures. Does it matter? I will say yes and no. No, the color of Yeshua is not an issue because we worship God in spirit, and the spirit does not have any color. However, the color of our Messiah matters for the sake of some people's history and identity.

Today, we understand that many things were altered and hidden to keep some of us ignorant. That's why it's very important to come together and share information. We can learn from each other.

How come Africans can be called savages because, in some parts of the continent, natives barely dress? Can you blame them in that heat? It is crucial to comprehend that individuals adjust to the circumstances and surroundings in which they reside. It will be absurd for someone in an area with temperatures above 90 degrees Fahrenheit (about 32 degrees Celsius) to wear a sweater or a coat.

Disparities ought not to hinder us from uniting and working together. Our Motherland is so beautiful, enriched with varied cultures, beliefs/traditions, communities, and resources. As a matter of fact, Africa is the most affluent continent globally, possessing all the essential elements required for the world to function properly.

Unfortunately, a false image was promoted, and today our continent is associated with poverty, ugliness, and violence.

What are we going to do about that?

Remember, if Africa falls, Everyone and Everything connected to her also falls.

TAKING ACTION

We've been thinking and doing the same things and obtaining the same results. It's time to change the way we think and do things to get different outcomes. Africa and her children are waking up. Now it's time to move forward with our true identity and get rid of the lies spread to keep us ignorant and in bondage.

I encourage my people to educate themselves and share the right information so they'll unite and not divide.

We should start seeing ourselves as a unified people living in different parts of the planet and having something special to share.

African nations need leaders that have Africa's best interests at heart. No more selling out.

Yes, we've been through a lot, but we are still here and stronger.

It's time to rise and take our rightful place, and to do that, we need to love each other.

Love is powerful. Our creator actually commanded us to love one another, but how can we do so if we don't know what love is or how love works?

Our creator talks about unselfish love, which means "*don't do to others what you don't want them to do to you or love your neighbor as you love yourself.*" Very powerful! Unity without love will make it very difficult for people to move forward, so it will be impossible to build together.

Acting out of selfless love entails prioritizing the well-being of those you live with or your community. Our personal interests will be satisfied when we seek each other's best interests. There will always be someone to see that another succeeds. And that will bring stability.

The best way to do that is to have a common goal. And our common goal here is what brings us together. What we have in common will bring us together. Our Motherland is the key to unlocking the door of our identity, acceptance, and love.

How can someone love others who look like them if they don't love what they see in the mirror?

How can someone love people that reflect what they don't like about themselves?

Anytime you see someone who reminds you of someone that you dislike, you'll tend to act a certain way toward that person if you're not strong enough to dissociate the two. Overcoming prejudices and past hurts may pose a challenge; however, we can make necessary changes with unwavering steadfastness and persistence.

If you don't love yourself or people who look like you, why do you want people to love and treat you well?

What kind of image are we showing the world? If we want to be loved, we must start loving each other. If we want to be respected, we must begin respecting each other. If we want to be accepted, we must start accepting each other. We have to change the way we do things.

What do we see around us? People from the same nation are fighting against each other because of tribal, religious, political, and social differences. They all look alike, but the hatred is so intense that instead of coming together to build, they link to fight and destroy.

That won't take us anywhere. The proof is all over. Look at what hatred and division have accomplished so far in people's lives!

We should remember that love attracts love, respect attracts respect, and hatred attracts hatred. People reap what they sow.

Knowing our identity, we must learn to accept and love ourselves. That healing process will help us overcome many wrong things done to our people.

When you tell a child or someone that they are not smart enough or beautiful, they will end up believing it and have very low self-esteem. That's, unfortunately, what most nations think about Africa and melanated people. How do we change that?

First, we have to know who we are and our own story, then accept our true identity so that we can stop seeing ourselves through everybody else's eyes and criteria. It is vital to reconnect with our source and our values. No tree can stand with no roots in a storm. The storm is what many go through in life. It can be social injustice, racism, violence, wars, slavery, colonization, division, etc.

A COMMON GOAL

It's possible to unite and work together as long as we focus on a common goal that will benefit all.

It's like a soccer, basketball or baseball game. Supporters come together despite their differences to see their team win. In our case, Africa is our team, and our shared goal is the African Renaissance.

We can at least agree that we all come from Africa, especially the ones with more melanin. So let's play or work together for Africa to win. Some are players, and others are supporters. You don't necessarily have to be a part of a team to be a supporter. Some may want to be supporters because they hate all forms of injustice or are humanitarians, and others may be supporters because they're disciples of Yeshua/Jesus or religious. Some may also want to support the cause simply because they're African or their ancestors are from Africa.

Whatever the reason, you want The Motherland to stand and take her rightful place.

And if we want Africa to have the place that she deserves, some perceptions have to change.

Let's take two children of African descent whom we'll call child 1 and child 2.

We teach child 1 that his/her ancestors came from Africa, a wonderful continent with great people, and so on. Amidst the conflicts, many were forcibly removed from their homes, and due to a lack of proper education, their value as invaluable treasures was not recognized. Consequently, despite their inherent beauty, strength, and uniqueness, they were subjected to mistreatment.

On the other hand, you tell child 2 that his/her ancestors came from Africa, a laid-back, dirty continent with uncivilized people that need help. Some were sold by their own people, and so on. Some people said that they were cursed and ugly.

How do you think that child 2 will behave? Will he/she be proud of that African culture? I don't think so. They will try to completely separate themselves from those ugly and cursed people who sold their ancestors, while child 1 will have a particular interest in the culture of their ancestors from Africa. Child 1 will have higher self-esteem than child 2, especially if the last one resembles the people of Africa.

We cannot blame either of them. Most people tend to try to forget hurtful and shameful situations or try to disconnect from the pain. Most people want to be accepted. Child 2 will disconnect from Africa to be accepted. Have you ever heard the expression "*guilty by association?*" Africa has been linked to a bad and false image causing many people to reject the ones associated with the Motherland.

What kind of story do you want to tell your child? What kind of education do you want your children to have?

It's time to take charge of our destiny. We're ambassadors of Africa to the world. We have to represent the Motherland very well.

We have to retell our story and re-educate ourselves based on real facts. We have to understand instead of judging. We have to accept instead of rejecting. We have to redefine beauty and values.

We see God in His creatures. We're all beautiful because we are the image of God, and God does not have any color. In fact, we are spiritual beings living in physical bodies, which connect us to this material world. We were sent to this world by God according to the mission He wants us to accomplish. Our body is our work equipment. Remember that your purpose is hidden in your Identity. It is very important not to judge or mistreat people based on their racial figures, tribe, or origin.

Anyone doing that is fighting against God's purpose for that person. People judge God by doing so, and God has a purpose for everyone. We are all on a special mission. We just have to find out what that special mission is. No matter what our religion, race, gender, and origin are, we'll have to give an account to our creator.

That's why it is vital to know and understand your identity. We must help each other succeed instead of putting stone blocks on each other's paths.

TEAMWORK

Teamwork is very important to build together. Being a part of a society is not enough to achieve a common goal. Most of the time, more is better than one because diverse skills are used to enhance productivity. Working together as a team can be pretty challenging.

Some people are wolves in sheep's clothing. They are good at pretending. Watch out!

Know who your enemies are. A particular race is not your enemy, nor is a tribe or a country. Your enemy is anyone who does not want you to succeed and steals your peace. Know how to choose your team or partners.

Your enemies may not be as far away as you think. They can be in your homes, schools, or work. They can be where you least expect. They can be everywhere. Be careful not to share everything with everybody.

People must be qualified to have access to certain things in your life. We don't share everything with everybody. Some people are "dream killers." They'll give some advice based on their fears and failures. Be careful. Fear paralyzes. It's an enemy of growth and can push you to make irrational decisions.

Can you imagine a child being afraid to walk because they fell once or twice while trying to walk? Fear is an enemy of destiny. Not only will it stop you or slow you down, but it will also affect your physical health. A positive mindset is a must. Be confident.

You need to be around positive people because moods and mindsets are contagious. As I said earlier, people are usually influenced by what they see or hear. So if you want to grow in a particular area of your life, be around people who can pour knowledge into you.

No one can give what they do not have.

If you want to progress in a particular area, find individuals who have achieved success in that area. They can provide invaluable insights from their personal journey and the obstacles they overcame. By sharing their perspective as winners, they can motivate and inspire you.

However, an eagle that spends too much time with chickens may begin to see itself as one of them.

A chicken cannot teach an eagle how to fly or be an eagle. Remember, you cannot give what you don't have, and you want to be a capital asset to your team or society. Everyone wants to succeed, and success has some requirements.

VALUES

First of all, it is vital to understand the times we're living in.

What do we do in a society where things move so fast?

It is a new era; technology is everywhere. News and information move faster than before. All aspects of life are affected. How do we cope with that?

People want things faster. Unfortunately, corrupted minds want things faster at any cost with less or no effort.

It's okay to want things faster and better, but not at any cost or in any way.

Good values are fundamental and determinant.

Your values will determine how you live and do things.

What is value?

Value is like a house built on a rock. The rock has to be strong enough to hold the house steady when the storm comes. The house can be shaken but won't fall. People may be tempted to do certain things or act a certain way in times of trouble, but with solid values, they will stay faithful to the education they received. Values are rooted in education, which shapes one's outlook on life. A high-quality education plays a decisive role in establishing stable and prosperous nations.

We cannot talk about strong nations without talking about families' welfare.

Parents and communities have to do their parts. We need role models and good leaders at the head of our communities and nations. In most cases, leaders are the reflection of their communities, and communities are the reflection of most families. Not to say the least, children are usually the mirror of their families.

Confused or unstable families frequently produce unstable communities and nations.

To surmount this challenge, we must identify our foundation. What is your bedrock? What educational foundation supports your values and worldview? To address these inquiries, we must acknowledge the central role that families play in a community.

People interact with each other since they live in the same environment. As a matter of fact, It's challenging for people with different values to live peacefully or build together. That's where educational institutions play an essential role. Hence, the importance of schools is to give a common education and understanding in order to build a community or nation. Families also play a vital role in the education system since the first years of a child's life are said to be the most crucial, as personality and morale are mainly shaped during that time.

Stable families produce healthier communities and stronger systems.

The right mindset is very important. Communities need role models or mature people willing to train or transfer their knowledge and experiences to future generations and anyone willing to grow.

How do we train someone?

There are different ways to train someone. The education that a child receives at home is fundamental. Parents are responsible for giving their children the best education they can. And to do that, they have to provide a safe and stable environment for their family. It's vital for a child to feel loved and secure. Children learn a lot through observation, and adults have to be more careful about what they do or say around them. Because they are more vulnerable, they need to be protected.

Schools also play an essential role in the training process. Parents cannot do it alone because their children are part of the community in which they live. They have to learn to work with others as they follow the same rules and laws required by the system to build a healthy society.

Rules and laws are made so people can live together in a disciplinary and respectful community. But everything starts at home.

Religion and social media also influence our values.

Religion affects the way people perceive things and behave. Most religions teach good values.

Social media is also influencing the way people perceive things. New technology, information, music, and entertainment reach our homes faster than before and children are exposed to more than they should. We have to adapt and move forward. Remember, our children have to be protected.

A SYSTEM

We are victims of a system that does not work for us; a system imposed or inherited through slavery and colonization. We have not been made for that system. What do we mean by "system"?

A system can be defined as a mechanism or a set of rules designed to accomplish a goal; systems frame how people see the world. Imposing a particular system on groups unfamiliar with it may be challenging.

What's going on in many African nations proves that the system does not work. Wars, fights, divisions, and hatred are weakening our Motherland. Too much power is given to the wrong people. We need to stop comparing Africa to other continents. Africa has her own stories and realities. She was compelled to adopt a system that was alien to her culture, and her offspring now grapple with unfamiliar codes of conduct that are challenging and often misconstrued. Let's not forget that a great number of Africans living on the continent are not "educated" or trained for that new system, and all that brings confusion. Africa became disconnected from her source, her identity, and her reality. No one can adequately adapt if they don't really understand what is expected of them. Communication is essential, and good communication is based on mutual respect. We may not agree on everything, but let's try at least to respect each other's opinions and cultures.

Frustrated people are often suscep-tible to being more violent. You can-not oppress and expect acceptance or peace. We must understand that na-tions were built on different values and traditions; people are unique. We have to accept differences instead of reject-ing unfamiliarity. That system won't work for us as long as we are going to be disconnected from our values and cultures. To avoid conflicts, a system that works for everyone to accomplish a set goal must be based on mutual respect and acceptance. We don't ex-pect everyone to love us, but we must be respected. We'll have to be more tolerant if we are going to work and live together.

It's time to change things. What do people expect when they oppress or mistreat others?

RESPECT

Respect is paramount. It is a positive feeling or high esteem towards someone, usually followed by positive actions. Respect is impossible without admiration. Self-respect is a prerequisite for respecting others. No one can offer what they lack. Change starts with us. Before trying to change or judge others, we first need to check ourselves. We cannot expect people to do what we refuse to do. Change is work, as it takes time, effort, and perseverance. Everything starts with a will. We choose to change.

There is a difference between respect and fear. Respect comes from admiration, while fear comes from terror.

Admiration is not love but can lead to love. Admiration is a social emotion felt by observing or hearing about people, while love is a strong feeling of affection toward someone or something. We usually love someone for who they are and admire someone for what they do.

People may not love you for who you are because of your origin, and that's okay because you cannot change your DNA, but you can change how they perceive you and your heritage.

People respect what they admire. You don't beg or ask for respect. You get it; not by force but by work. Your work or your fruit shows who you are and what you can do. The ancient Egyptians were held in high esteem for their achievements, and to this day, the pyramids continue to astonish people.

Your work proves who you are, so if you want to change things in your life, you must change how you do things. You cannot quit when things don't work at first. Have you heard about the famous saying *"quitters never win"*? We cannot let discouragement or fear stop us from progressing. People are usually affected by what they see or hear, and if we want to be respected, we have to start by knowing who we are as we accept and love our true identity. People respect and protect what they love.

Yes, indeed, they usually fight for what they value in life. We have to protect and cherish our communities and our nations. It's essential to work for the stability and development of our countries.

We shouldn't always wait for people to do things for us. The hand that asks depends on the hand that gives. Independence, or freedom, starts with our mind. In fact, poverty is in the mind. A person can be surrounded by wealth and still be poor. It's a mindset issue. Change starts from within. But you have to know what you want.

A clear vision will help you move forward in life. Confusion paralyzes and stops people from making progress. That's a form of bondage. No one can make any progress in bondage. Many Afro-descendants are confused because they're disconnected from their source and traditions. Wearing someone else's shoes may not help you reach your destination because people have different purposes. Wrong assignments bring confusion, and everyone has a specific mission on earth.

Your origin, culture, and identity are parts of your equipment to accomplish that mission.

A negative image of yourself is another form of bondage. Why do I say that? A negative self-perception will stop you from achieving much. That's why it is imperative to change that false and bad image given to Africa and anyone or anything associated with her. Africa, the mother of humanity, is just misunderstood. Accepting Africa means accepting and embracing your true self. Rejecting Africa means denying who you are. Africa is where everything started and will end.

Africa is everywhere.

REPROGRAMMING

It's never easy to reprogram oneself. In fact, change can be painful since it requires some sacrifices. Not to say the least, changing old habits can be challenging. We have to be willing to make any change that will help us move forward.

It may be uncomfortable at first, but you have to be persistent even if you make some mistakes along the way. Everybody makes mistakes. The difference is that some people learn from them, and some don't. How can one expect different results from doing the same thing with the same mindset?

The same cause produces, most of the time, the same results.

It's okay to make some mistakes as long as we learn from them. That's how we mature and make better decisions in life.

Experiences will affect our thinking and choices in life.

They can be positive or negative. The most important thing is to apply what we have learned effectively.

Adverse experiences may leave severe damage that can hinder our progress in life.

It's essential not to let negative experiences or mistakes stop us from achieving our goals.

Unfortunately, unpleasant experiences can leave some very deep wounds, which can take longer to heal and slow growth.

Healing can take time. It's a process. Hurt people usually hurt others, with a few exceptions.

It's important to be at peace with one-self.

Being at peace is a good indication that one is on the right track. Finding your purpose in life is a must. Success is achieved when you fulfill the purpose for which you were created.

The decisions that we make influence our life and those around us. As your perception of life changes, your be-havior will also change.

Behaviors are learned, so they can be altered.

Our mind works like a computer. We have to deprogram and reprogram our mindset.

Reprogramming yourself can be challenging, but possible. A strong will and determination are a must. The rest will follow. Just remember that there is a champion living inside of you.

We have to reprogram ourselves, which means having a different mindset. To have a new mindset, we have to delete useless things or the old mindset that was keeping many under bondage.

What do we mean by bondage? Bondage is anything that slows us down or stops us from being productive and at peace. Being prosperous does not fall from the sky.

We have to be willing to invest in ourselves and strive for excellence so that we can be more fruitful. Personal development is very important. No one can give what they don't have. It is very important to add value to oneself, not only because nowadays the world is very competitive but because we want to bring something to the table. People who don't bring much to the table are not highly valued. We live in a world that highly values people who can bring things to the table. In one word, you have to do your part since you are part of a community. Things, except miracles, don't just happen like that. And as a part of a team, you want to be involved. Some people don't get involved because they think they don't have much to add. If you don't value yourself, you will be limited in what you can do. Just look within yourself. There is something that you do naturally, and you feel peace. Something may be burning inside of you, but you are being hesitant because you feel incapable of doing it. Who told you that it was not for you? You may not be ready, which doesn't mean it's not for you. Get ready. Fight for what you believe. Let your dream be a reality. If not, you won't feel fulfilled. Find your divine mission on earth. There is something in you that is needed in your home, in your family, community, and nation.

Understanding one's role and what is expected of them in order to move toward a common goal is important. We must have a common goal to advance together; if not, complications such as division and strife may occur.

"No one can follow two masters. Two people cannot walk together unless they agree. A double-minded person cannot receive anything from God." Some religious books even teach the fundamental truth about agreement. Confusion and division hinder people from reaching a common goal or living peacefully together.

Together, we can build stronger nations, despite our different religious beliefs, social classes, backgrounds, or origins.

We are living together, so let's make things work.

It's time to change!

PRACTICAL ADVISES/ CONCLUSION

Know what you want in life and move forward. Plan accordingly. It will be difficult to meet your goals with no plan. Don't just do things to do them or because it works for someone else. You may not have the same purpose in life. Find what works for you. Be original. Do you know your talents and gifts? You must be good at something! Find it! There is something that comes naturally. What do you enjoy doing? Remember, there is a champion living inside of you! Let him/her out!

Stay focused. Distraction can keep you from accomplishing your goals on time, and time is valuable. Everything has its time and season. You have to discern which season of your life you are in. What do I mean by that?

You don't expect to reap when it's time to sow. It may be a time in your life when you need to build yourself up or get more knowledge before jumping into a particular field or situation. It may also be a time when you need to be by yourself for a little while to hear God's voice, refocus, or heal. Healing is essential. Most hurt people hurt others. Pain can blur your vision and affect the decisions you are making. Pain can also lead to fear, which can paralyze you. Yes, being afraid to go through what did not work before. That might not have been the right time for it. Don't be afraid to trust again or start over! Healing is a process, and it requires time. Make sure to properly heal before jumping into anything else too soon. Take your time to do things right.

Don't be intimidated by others. No matter what has happened in the past, keep your head up. Don't live in the past. The past is gone. What are you doing today? Work on yourself and build your tomorrow wisely.

Have the right mindset to succeed. Don't always look for mistakes in people's lives or be a fault-finder. Blaming anything or everyone else for not doing what you know you're supposed to be doing won't take you very far. Finding excuses for not succeeding will not help you much, either. On the other hand, a victorious mindset will help you overcome every obstacle and opposition you may be facing. Some situations are sometimes there to make you stronger and wiser. Have the right attitude and trust God.

What do you see when you look at yourself in the mirror?

Doing the same thing produces the same result.

We need the right mindset to build solid and healthy nations. It's time to change the way we've been thinking and doing things. It's time to rise and shine. It's time to reconnect to our roots and let our identity shine. Everyone has a specific task to accomplish. We just have to find our purpose—everyone has a particular assignment, and we have to find it to stay connected to our purpose for being on earth. Our creator does not make any mistakes. We also have to be more tolerant of each other and accept to work with our differences; that will make us stronger. Let's face it! We need each other, so let's make wise or positive decisions.

What do you see when you look at yourself in the mirror?

It's time to change!

No part of this publication may be reproduced, translated, stored in or introduced into a retrieval system, or transmitted, in any form or by any means (electronic, mechanical, photocopying, recording, or otherwise) without permission in writing or prior notice from the author. Copyright 2019.

NOTE

NOTE

NOTE